Bushcraft And Survival Deadfall Traps

Disclaimer: The information contained within this book is strictly for educational purposes. If you wish to apply ideas contained in this book, you are taking full responsibility for your actions.

Contents

In a survival situation or whilst practicing bushcraft, the ability to make traps will make sure you never go hungry, people all over the world have made traps to get food for thousands of years and no doubt deadfall traps were used extensively . this book will show you a few different deadfall traps you can make and use in a survival situation or whilst practicing bushcraft if local laws allow their use, whether you can use them or not it's a great skill to practice anyway, especially knowing many of our ancestors would have used such things on a daily basis.

To make most of the traps mentioned it will be easier if you have modern tools like a knife, saw, axe etc but with practice you should be able to make most of them with primitive tools like our ancestors would have done.

Reverse figure 4 deadfall

The reverse figure 4 can be a bit fiddly to set up but it's worth practicing making it, you may need a knife to make it because like the ordinary figure 4 it requires quite a few different notches and cuts to make it, but if you practice enough you may be able to make it with primitive tools.

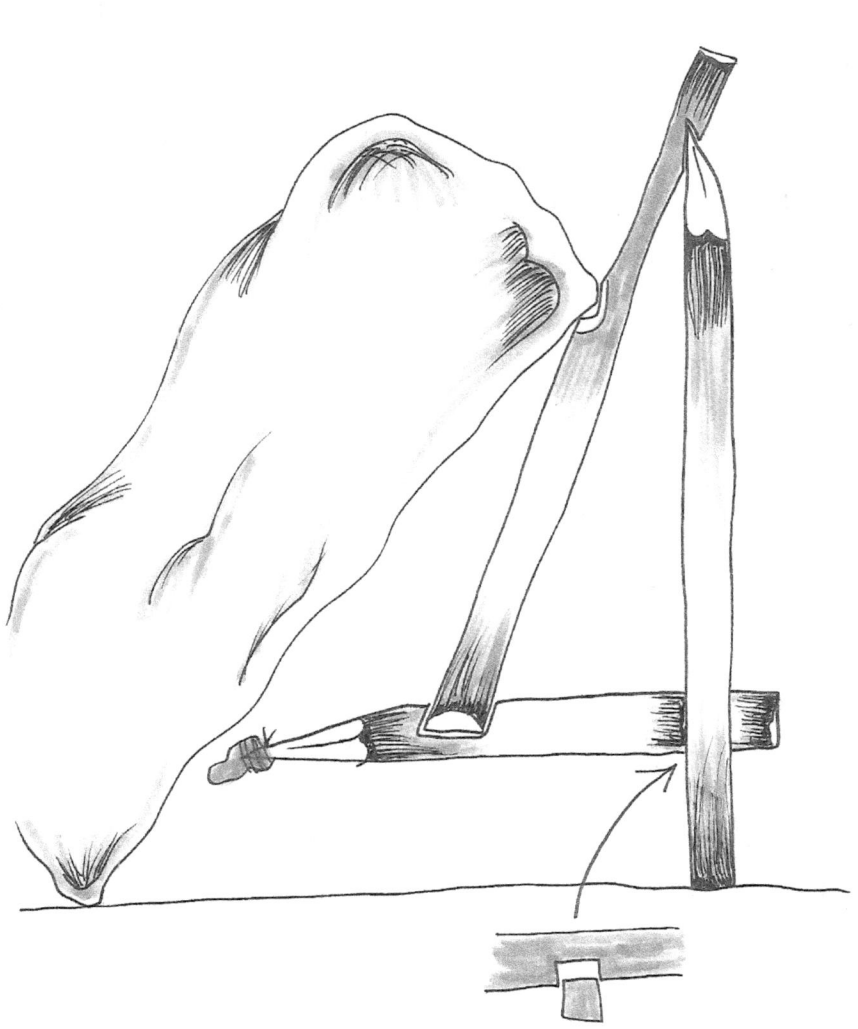

Reverse figure 4 deadfall

The reverse figure 4 is very much like the 3 stick deadfall trigger but with a few more cuts/notches and very similar to the ordinary figure 4 but set the other way around and with the bait /trigger stick extended at the back end, when the bait stick is pressed down it releases the other parts of the trigger and down comes the weight, to make it follow the instructions for the figure 4 (next chapter) but make the back notch of the bait /trigger stick more square and the back end of the slanting stick square instead of a flat point and extend the back of the bait stick to your required length, the only other notch you have to make is a small notch in the slanting stick to help hold up your weight.

Figure 4 deadfalls

Figure 4 deadfall trap triggers require more carving than most other triggers but if made properly they will be a very effective trap trigger and can be made bigger or smaller depending on the animal . Depending on what type of figure 4 you are making a knife/saw will definitely make things much easier, but it can be made using flint tools, to make the split log version you will need an axe, a saw and a knife .

Figure 4 split log trap

flat wood figure 4

Figure 4 with top stick made from a curved /
bent stick

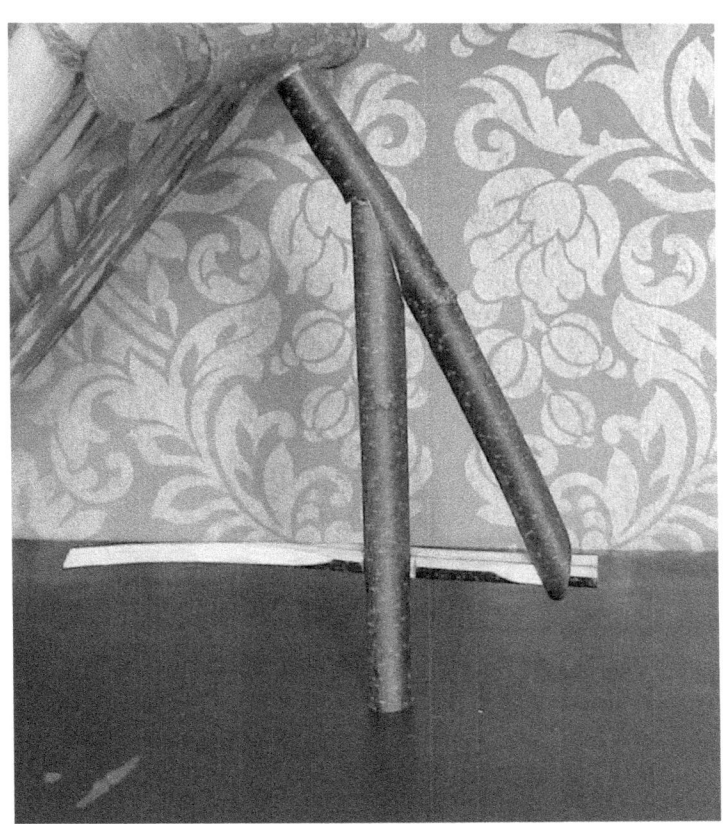

Simple figure 4

Close up of the notches
From left to right : slanting stick,
upright/vertical stick and horizontal
stick/trigger stick

Figure 4 deadfall

As you can see from the pictures there are quite a few different ways to make the figure 4 trigger and numerous ways of the setting them up as traps. all the triggers require the central 2 sticks that cross over to be able to lightly lock together and the top one locks into the back of the horizontal stick whilst pivoting on the top of the upright stick. A simple way to make it is as follows,

The upright stick and the trigger / bait stick need to have 2 square notches cut into it so they fit together as pictured then cut the top of the upright stick to a flat point, then at the outside end of the trigger stick you have to cut a notch into it to accept the back end of the slanting stick, the other end of the trigger can have notches cut in to make bait tying easier, now put the upright stick and the trigger stick on the floor together how they would be set, now lay your slanting stick where it's meant to go and mark the areas to cut a flat point at one end (to fit into the back end of trigger stick) and another cut to fit it to the top of the upright stick, hopefully the pictures will make sense of it, don't make everything really tight otherwise the trap may not go off when the trigger is touched, the bait is tied to the trigger to make it so the animal will have to pull and chew to get the bait off .

3 stick deadfall

The 3 stick deadfall is a relatively easy trap to make, you simply need 3 sticks to make it. A knife will make things easier but it's not always needed to make this trap. Snapping sticks will do the job and ends can be flattened with a stone and a notch can be cut with a flint flake .

Simple 3 stick deadfall with logs as the weight

3 stick deadfall

3 STICK DEADFALL TRAP

3 balanced sticks hold a deadfall weight up, the weight is pushing onto one stick that is held back and in place by the others, when an animal takes the bait it will release the other sticks and bring the deadfall down. Take 3 sticks each roughly half the size of each other, some of your sticks may need to be cut to fit, put some bait on the smallest stick now cut a small notch as shown in the middle size stick at one end to fit the other stick into it. then place the upright longest stick at an angle and put the middle stick in place and hold with 1 hand near the top, now place the deadfall on the middle size stick as shown, place the bait stick between the 2 other sticks, make sure the longest stick is positioned so it is not under the deadfall otherwise it may get stuck. The upright stick if well back can be pushed into the ground to stop it falling backwards.

Paiute deadfall

Another old trap which works very good, you may need to make some string for it, but it would be worth it in the end, it goes off at the slightest touch but will hold a fairly big weight . You can make this trap without any tools if you have to but you will need some sort of cordage, if you can make it use natural cordage or a shoelace would do the trick.

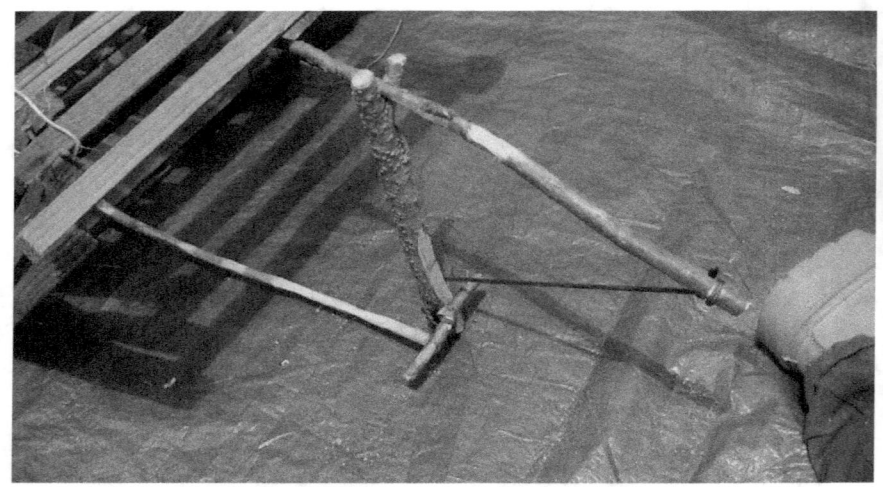

Forked top paiute

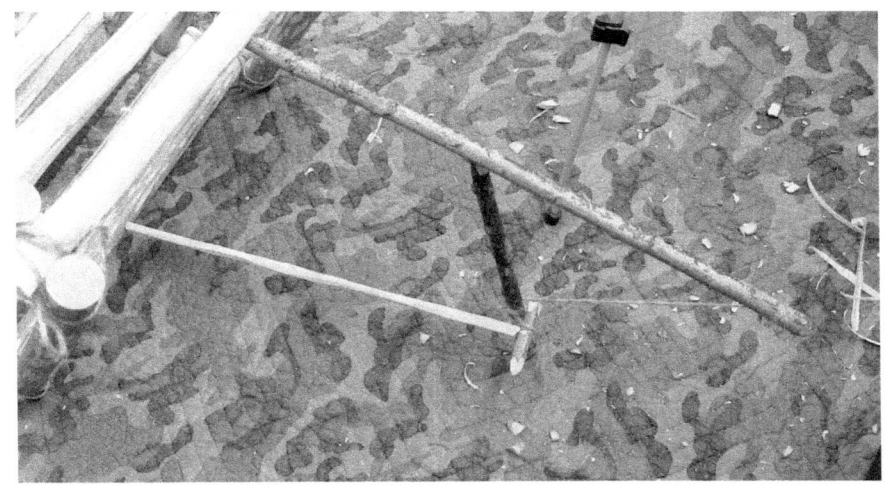

Paiute deadfall

The paiute deadfall trap will require string, 2 medium sized sticks, a long stick and a small toggle stick, the upright stick has a stick balancing on top of it which holds the weight at one end and has a string on the other end with a toggle attached, this toggle is wrapped around the upright stick and held in place by the trigger/bait stick when the animal steps on the trigger it releases the toggle and down comes the weight / deadfall. To make it first the upright stick is carved to a flat point at the top, then the top stick is placed onto it so that it pivots, then a mark is made where the ideal pivoting point is and a small notch is cut there, at the other end to where the weight will sit tie a string and take the string from the top stick to the upright stick near the bottom, now mark this and tie a small toggle here, now a long thin stick is placed between the back of the deadfall and the toggle, bait is placed on or near the trigger stick, and when an animal stands on it, it releases the trigger and the deadfall comes down.

Figure 9 deadfall

Only 2 sticks are required to make this trap trigger, one will need a small fork at one end and the other will need to be curved or bendable . A knife would make this trap easier to make but is not always needed, all parts could be snapped from a fresh stick, if the bent stick will not stay bent you will need a fire or heat to bend it into shape, but if you don't have a fire going you can tie it with string to hold it place .

Simple tied figure 9 deadfall

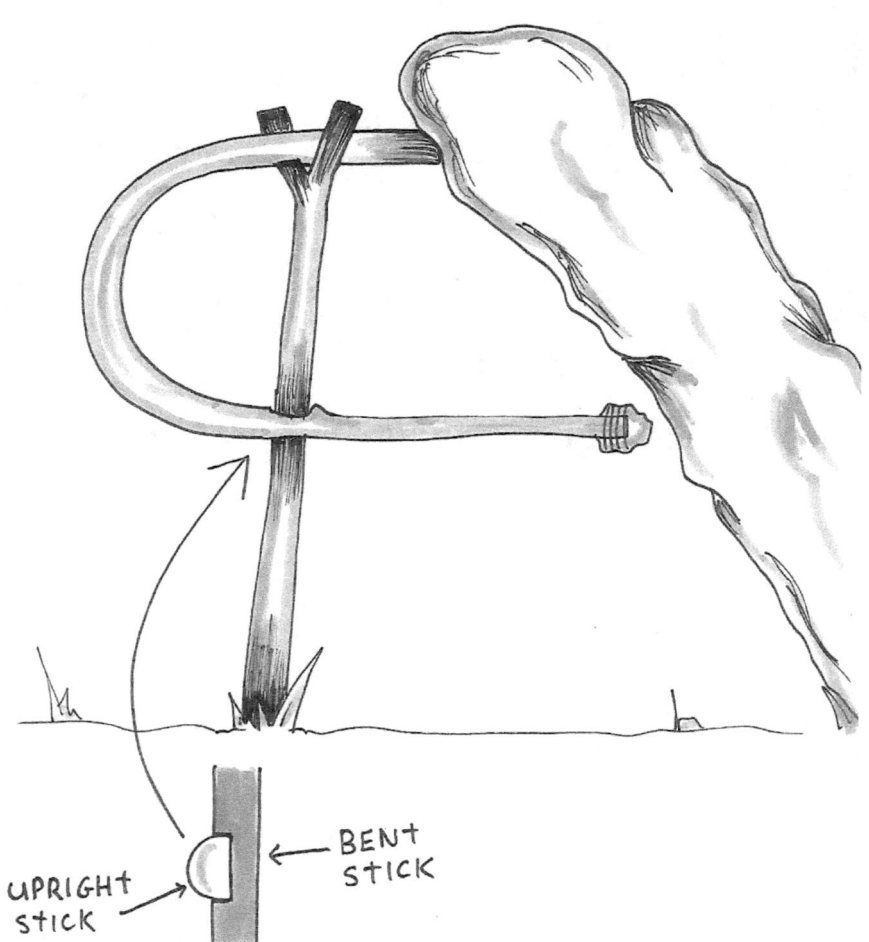

UPRIGHT
stick

BENt
stick

Figure 9 deadfall

The figure 9 deadfall works much like a figure 4 but you only need a curved stick and a straight stick , if you have a curved stick that will stay bent it will work fine without having to do anything extra, if your curved stick won't stay bent then you can either heat it over a fire or tie it in place with a string . bait is placed on the end of the bottom of the curved stick, when the bait is taken it dislodges the curved stick and flips it out of the way and the weight comes down. The upright stick and the curved stick will need slight notches cut into them just like a figure 4. To make it, take a stick with a small fork one end and cut it to the height of what you want the deadfall to sit, half way down it cut a square notch, now take a bendy stick and bend it or heat it till its bend and place it as pictured, cut a small notch to fit it into the upright stick and keep it in place, now trim off any bits that are too long and add your bait to the end of the bottom curved stick as shown . If the curved stick slip back at the another small square notch could be cut to hold it in place better .

String tension deadfall

A fairly simple trap, you will need string, a log, a few twigs, and a nearby tree. Some strong string will be needed if you intend to use a very heavy deadfall weight, if you can find a log of the right size you may not need a saw or knife as the rest of the parts could be snapped sticks and flattened with flint or a coarse stone.

String tension deadfall

The string tension deadfall works by having a log suspended over a nearby tree branch with a string that goes down to a trigger of 3 sticks, the string is wrapped around 2 of the sticks as shown in the picture, when the middle stick is dislodged it releases the string and down comes the deadfall weight, to make it start by tying a string to a log and throwing the string over a suitable branch, then 2 sticks are pushed in the ground as shown and a 3rd stick is placed on top of one upright stick and in front of the other, then the log is raised and the string is wrapped under the horizontal stick and around the upright, then then back down to the horizontal stick as shown in the pictures.

Samsons post deadfall

Once you have the parts to make this trap it is simple to set up, but to get all the parts especially for the log type samsons post you may need a saw to cut the bits to size especially if you want to make it from larger sized logs (unless you can find the right sized logs on the ground) the rest could be made using primitive tools

samsons post deadfall

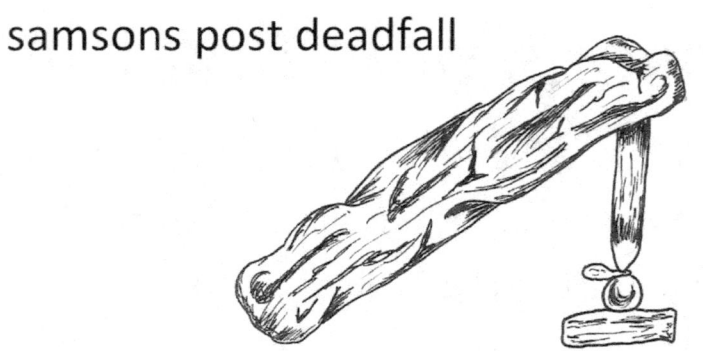

SAMSONS POST DEADFALL TRAP

A log is balanced on a 2 piece trigger consisting of an upright stick and small round (or half round) log on top of another (1 log split into 2 can also be used) the bait is placed between the 2 piece trigger and 2 or more sticks are used along the side to stop the log toppling off the other one, when the animal tries to take the bait it dislodges the upright stick and brings down the log on the top.

To make it first place 1 log on the floor push some sticks in the ground along the sides, then carve a stick with a blunt point, and place a small log or stone on the bottom log now place bait on the small log / stone and put the the upright stick in place, now put the top log carefully on the trigger, an alternative method is to use rocks instead of logs and a round stone instead of a small log for the trigger.

2 stick deadfall

A simple trap that can be made quickly, not as good as some of the others but is well worth trying, the good thing with this trap is it can be made by simply snapping 2 sticks to your required length

2 stick deadfall

2 STICK DEADFALL

A very simple trap using 2 sticks, an upright stick is balanced under another stick with a deadfall weight on top of it, bait is placed between the deadfall and the stick, when the animal tries to take the bait it will dislodge the trigger and be crushed under the deadfall.

To make it take 2 sticks one longer than the other and and tie some bait to smaller stick, now balance the 2 as shown making sure the upright stick is as far to the edge of the deadfall as will allow.

Split stick deadfall

A pretty decent trigger, it can be a bit fiddly to set up, but the trigger/bait stick does reach far under the deadfall, a knife or saw would make this trap easier to make but you can do it by snapping the sticks and flattening the ends with a coarse stone or flint and cutting in the small notch with a bit of flint or glass.

split stick deadfall

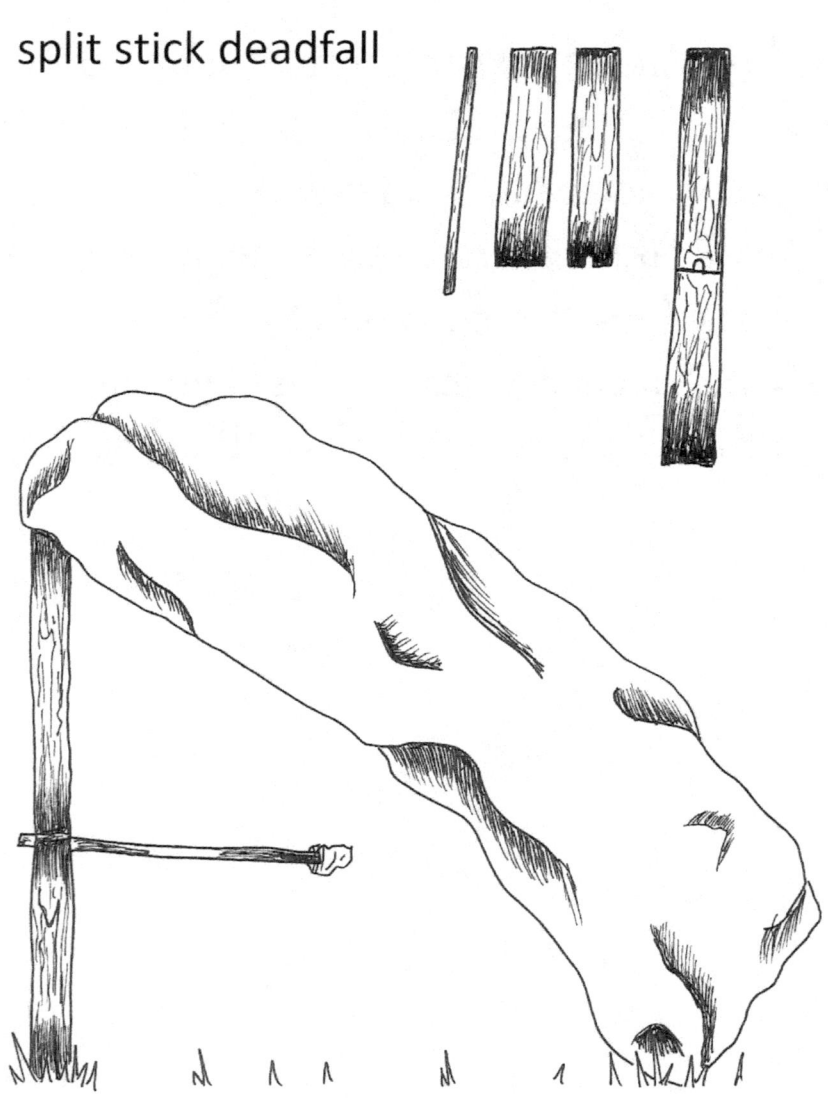

SPLIT STICK DEADFALL

A simple deadfall trap, the trigger is 2 bits of stick with a small groove carved into the top of the bottom stick and another smaller stick is placed into the groove between the 2 to act as a trigger / bait stick, an animal will push or nudge the stick and cause the 2 main sticks to come apart and the rock will fall. To make it take a strong stick and cut it in 2 at the middle, now carve a small groove into the end of one stick, then take a smaller stick and carve it to fit tightly into the groove, now put the 2 together with smaller stick between them and balance a large rock / log on top as shown in the picture.

Arapuca deadfall

In my opinion this is one of the best triggers around, not much carving is involved but the trap will go off at the slightest touch even from smaller animals, this trap can be made without a knife or saw quite easily, i have made many by simply snapping the twigs to size and making a small notch with a bit of flint or glass, sometimes you can do it without using a blade at all by using a stick with a small branch you can snap off and use that instead of a notch .

51

Arapuca deadfall

The arapuca deadfall trap is essentially the same as any other arapuca bird trap but with a single stick trigger instead of 2 . The trigger of the trap in the picture consists of 3 sticks, only 1 notch is required, the notch is carved into the vertical stick so the angled stick has a place to fit into to hold it up, this then holds the deadfall up, and this in turn is held up by the angled stick forcing it to be pushed forward, the vertical stick is held back by the stick at the bottom, which is angled towards the back of the deadfall weight.

This trap works when the animal stands on or knocks away the stick at the bottom and the deadfall will fall and crush the animal, bait can be tied to the trigger stick or placed under and around it.

To make it take 3 sticks, 2 roughly the same length and one much longer, measure your 2 smaller sticks by holding them together like in the picture to how high you want your deadfall to be then cut a notch into the middle of one and a flat point into the other so they fit as shown in the pictures, once these are set you can measure your bait / trigger stick, once you have done this set it in place to hold the deadfall up .

Tripwire deadfall

Another good trap trigger, where the trigger /tripwire reaches far under the trap and is simple to make, a shoelace, or natural cordage could be used if you have no proper cordage at hand and this trap is easier to make if you have a knife, a swiss army type knife with a saw would make this trap in no time at all, but you could still make it without one using flint or similar natural items.

tripwire deadfall

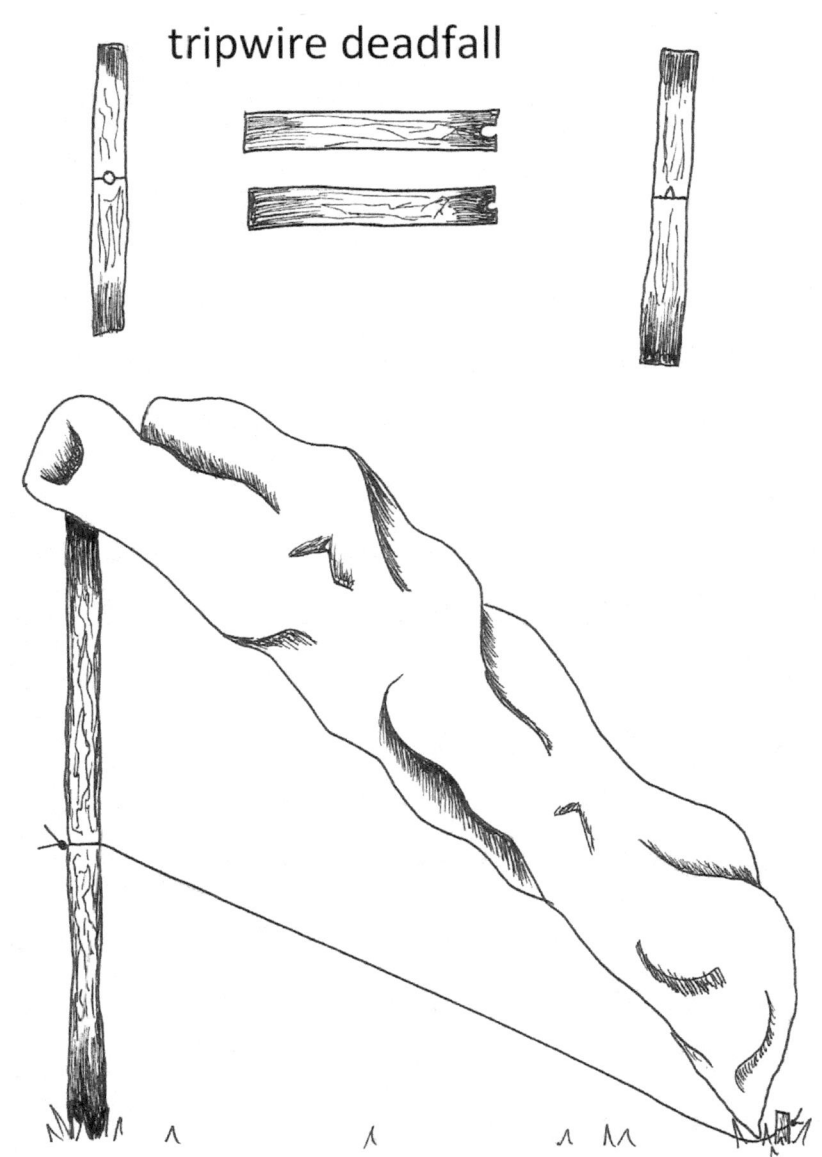

TRIPWIRE DEADFALL

A trap using 2 sticks with a string trigger, the string can either be through a groove in one stick with knot at the end or tied around one of them, the other end is tied to a small peg at the back of the deadfall, the animal dislodges the trigger when it steps on or nudges the string, bait could be tied to the string or placed at the back of the trap.

To make it take a stick and cut it in half and either carve a groove or or tie a string to the stick, if you choose the groove method, tie a large strong knot in the end of the string, now place the 2 sticks together with the string between and laid on the floor towards where the back of the deadfall is, now push a small peg into the ground and tie the other end of the string to this, now place your deadfall on to the sticks.

Split fork deadfall

A forked stick is all you really need to make this trigger, if you have no knife or saw you may be able to make the trigger by simply snapping the stick above the fork, but in an ideal world a small saw will make it much easier and more precise

split fork deadfall

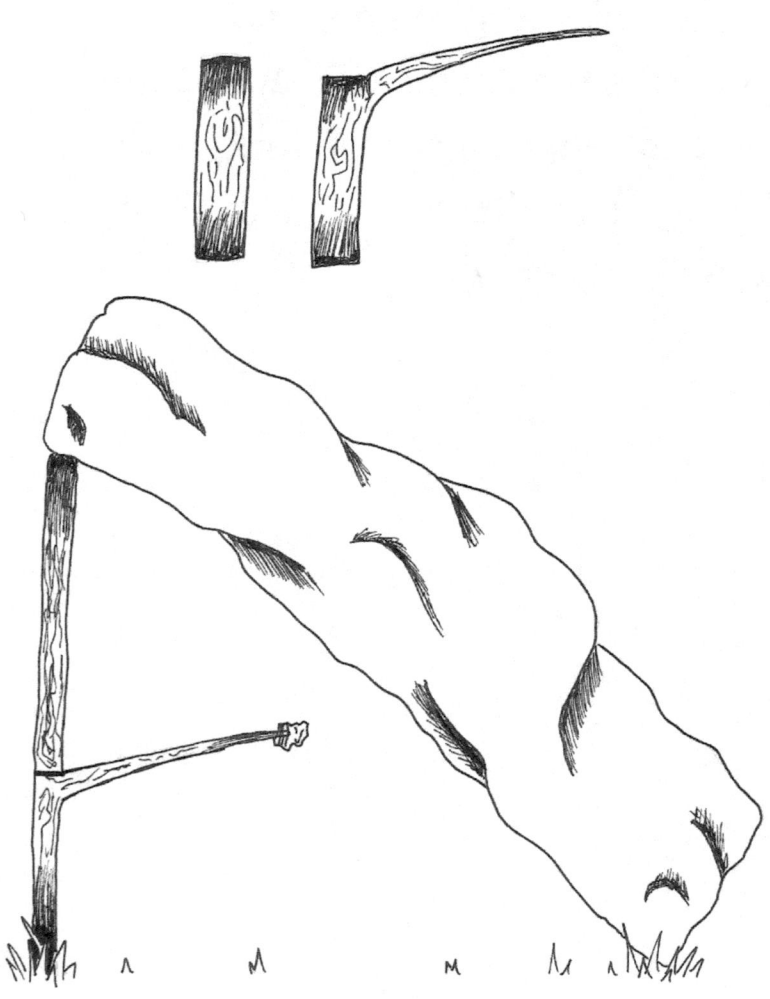

SPLIT FORK DEADFALL TRAP

This is a simple deadfall trap with a 2 piece trigger the animal attempts to take the Bait from the end of the stick and dislodges the trigger causing the deadfall weight to fall on top of the animal .

To make it first find a tree branch / stick with a side branch sticking out, shave the side branch to point, the stick is then cut in half just above the side branch as pictured and bait is placed on the end of the side branch, the 2 halves are placed together and a deadfall weight is placed on top.

Y stick deadfall

A forked stick and a few pebbles will be needed to make this trap . A bit of flint or glass can be used to point the ends if you have no knife with you.

y stick deadfall trap

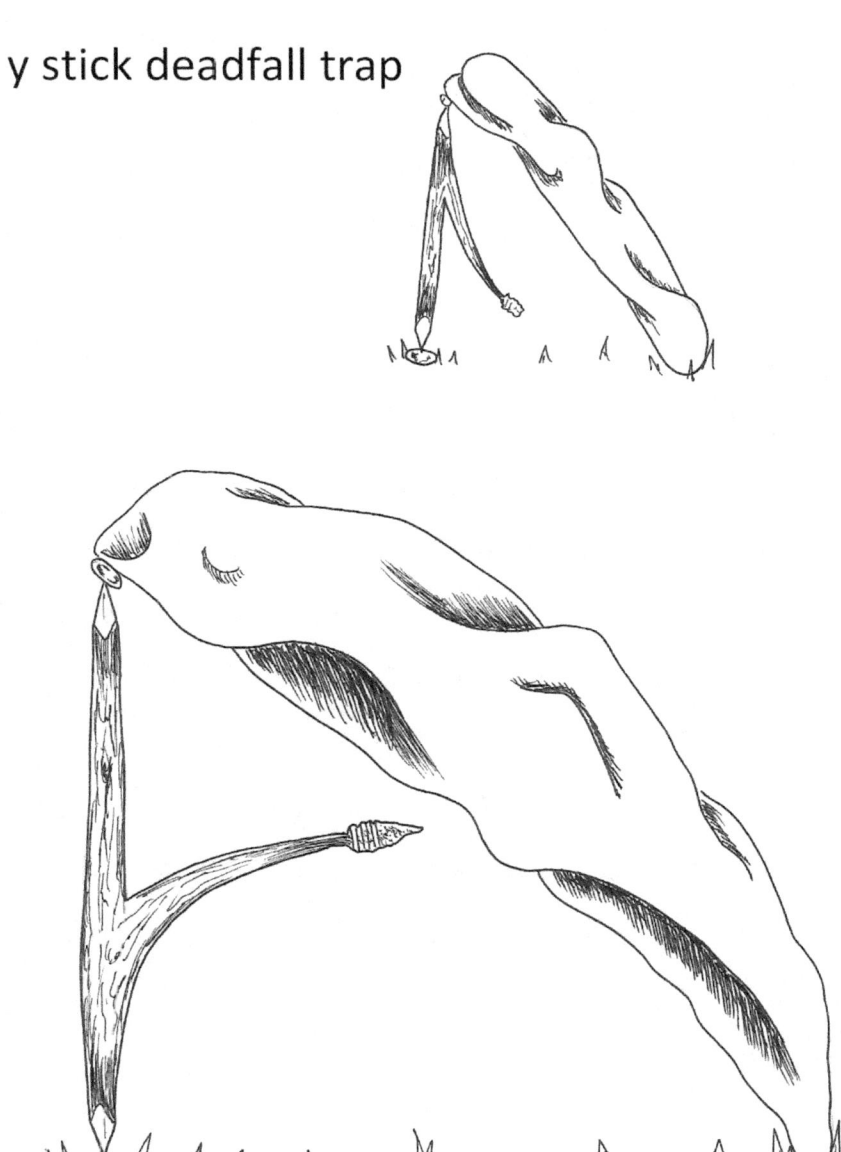

Y stick deadfall trap

This simple deadfall trap is made using a forked stick from a branch, when the animal tries to take the bait it will dislodge the trigger and bring the deadfall down on top of it.

To make it, find a forked stick and a deadfall weight and a few flat pebbles or bark etc, cut the fork as shown and to your required length and sharpen all ends of the fork points, now add your bait before setting it up, then put a flat pebble or something similar on the floor and place your trigger either way up (as shown) on the pebble, now balance the deadfall on the fork trigger, you can add another pebble at the top if required, but have the trigger as near to edge as possible.

Shoshone / pebble deadfall

A simple enough trap, some string is needed for this trap so natural cordage could be used or a shoelace, a flint flake can be used to point the ends of the stick if no other blades are available.

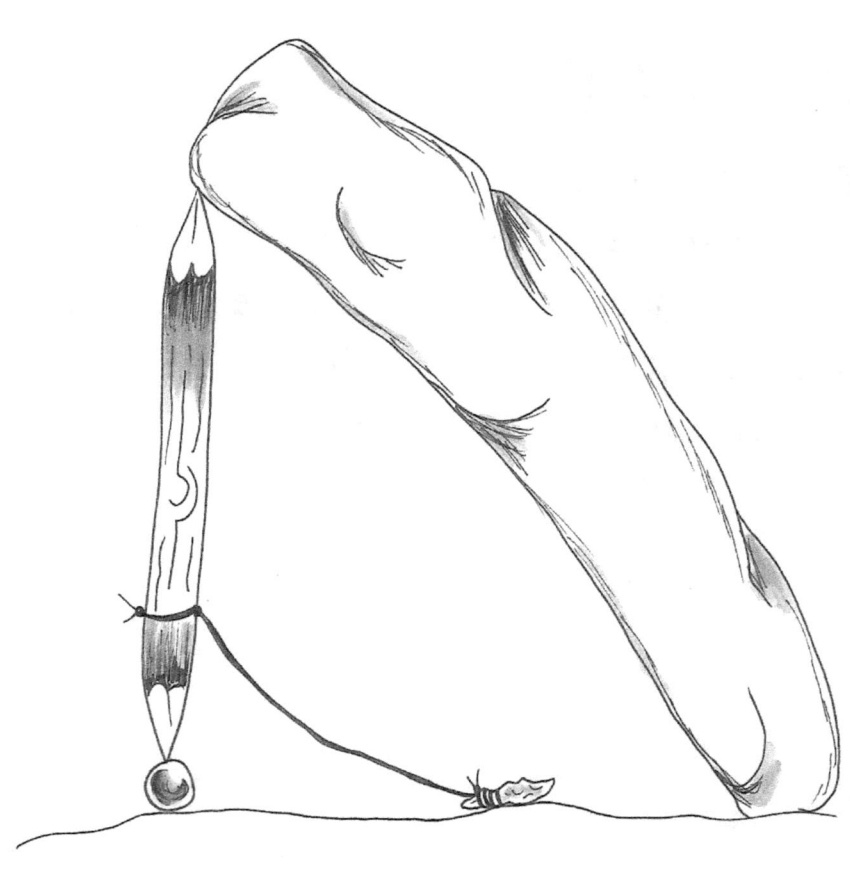

SHOSHONE / PEBBLE DEADFALL TRAP

Shoshone/pebble deadfall

This trap is a bit different from the others because it has the bait tied to a string and the upright stick is balanced on a small pebble to make it set off easier . Once the animal pulls the bait it will dislodge the stick from the pebble and down will come the deadfall weight.

To make it find a stick and carve both ends to a point and tie a string to the stick with bait on the end, now balance your stick on a round pebble and carefully place your deadfall weight on top. To stop the upright stick digging into the ground when the trap is set off you could place a flat rock under it and the pebble.

Pegged log deadfall

This trap will need to be placed near a tree to use a branch for your string / rope to pass over it and hold the log in place, you may need a knife for this trap because it requires a hole to be bored through a stick, otherwise you may have to rig something up like a bow drill to make the hole

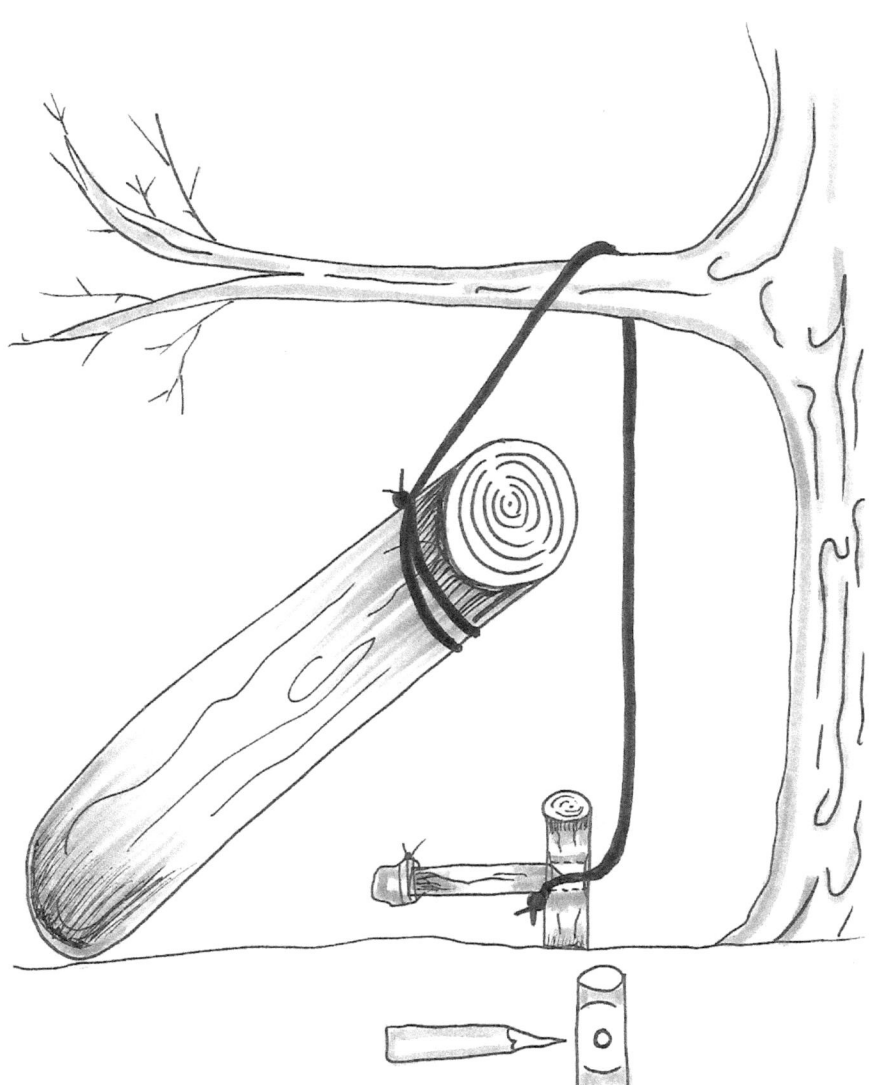

Pegged log deadfall

The log or deadfall weight on this trap is held up by a string passing through a hole bored through a stake that is hammered into the ground, the string has a knot tied at the end that passes through the hole and a small peg is inserted into the hole and stops the string from being pulled back through the hole, when the peg is dislodged it releases the knot tied on the string and down comes the deadfall weight.

To make it tie a string to your deadfall weight, throw the string over a branch and tie a knot in the end of the string, now bore a hole through a stake either with a knife / awl or a bow drill / hand drill set, and hammer the stake into the ground, make a small peg that will fit into the hole, but don't make it fit too tight, now pass the string with knot through the hole and gently plug the hole with the peg .

Old English deadfall trap

To make this trap trigger you will need a crooked stick, a forked stick, some string and a couple of straight sticks, you can also make this trap with a loop of string rather than a stick or just a single string with a loop tied at the end.

Old english deadfall trap

The deadfall weight is held up by a crooked stick that sits in the crotch of a forked stick, the crooked stick will want to flip up and drop the deadfall weight but a stick with notch is tied under the deadfall weight to a small peg, the end of the crooked stick sits in the notch of the tied stick and keeps it from flipping, when an animal stands on the stick it releases the crooked stick and down comes the deadfall weight . Bait goes on or around the bottom tied stick.

To make it hold your forked stick up against the deadfall and cut it to size, then cut your crooked stick slightly shorter and with a flat point at the end, now measure the bottom/ trigger stick and tie a string at one end and cut another flat notch in the other end, tie the end of that to a small peg pushed into the ground behind your deadfall weight, lift up the weight, put the fork in front of it and hold it up with the crooked stick, and place the end of the crooked stick in the flat notch of the bottom trigger stick, put bait around and under the bottom stick .

Deadfall weights

You may find in some areas you cannot find large rocks or logs to make the deadfall weight, but there are a few ways to get around this problem .

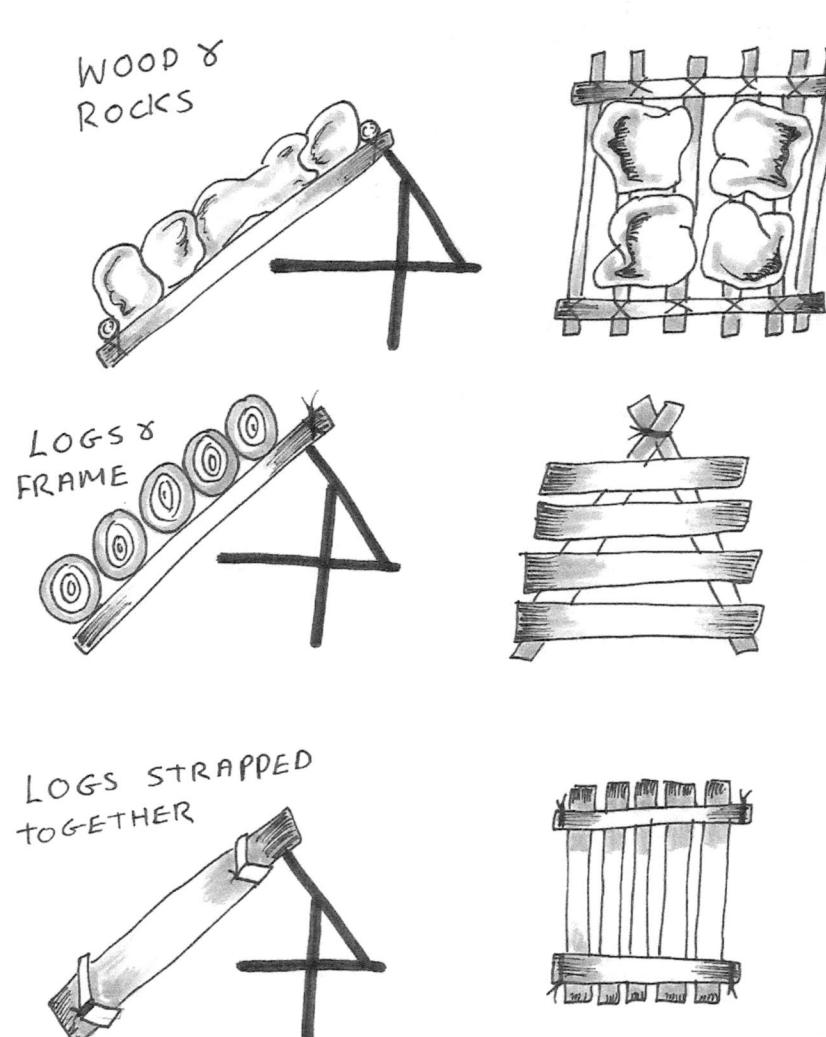

WOOD & ROCKS

LOGS & FRAME

LOGS STRAPPED TOGETHER

Deadfall weights

If you cannot find any large enough rocks or logs to make your deadfall weight you will have to make a frame of some sort or lash/tie smaller logs together, as you can see in the picture you can do this a few different ways, the top one is a frame with rocks laid on top of it, the middle one is a v shaped frame with logs tied or simply laid on the frame and the bottom is a row of logs tied together by putting a stick under and on top then tying them together to hold it all in place.

Many thanks for reading my book, i hope the info made sense, if you would like any further information check out my Youtube channel:
JJR SURVIVAL
15/5/2019

Also by the author :
Pheasant traps
Repurposed bushcraft equipment.
Bushcraft and survival hunting tools.
Basic survival traps.
Survival trapping, pheasant and ground bird traps.
How to make a natural slingshot
£160 bushcraft kit.
Practical homemade live traps
Simple mora knife modifications